RISE FROM FEAR TO COURAGE

Saddle Up and Enjoy Riding Your Horse Again!

ELISE HITTINGER

CONTENTS

INTRODUCTION

This is my story, my journey, my road to healing.

I was so excited to move onto our farm in Kentucky, being able to ride from the farm to the lake and ride around our property, that I didn't realize how much the fear from my accident had grown into a giant wall. We had built a ten-foot-wide path around the entire pasture, and we have a lot of trails already on our property with plans to make more.

There was no way I was going to let my fear of trail riding hold me back from enjoying our amazing property and all that Kentucky living has to offer. I went on a journey that I have described in this book. My journey is not over yet; in some ways, it is just beginning. The hardest thing was getting help for myself in my relationship with the horses.

Trainers just really didn't understand my fear. The personal coaches I could find really didn't understand horses, so I felt completely lost. I put a lot of this together on my own and found help here and there to create building blocks, a path to healing and courage. The journey isn't the same for everyone, the start is different, the path is different, the end results are different. What is the same is the decision, the "I want to enjoy being in the saddle again." That is the same for those of us who want to ride on our precious partners but are held back by fear. These are some of the tools that worked for me and my path.

DISCLAIMER

After a lot of trial and error, the author is giving you the best process that worked for her. The author accepts no responsibility or liability of any kind for any actions or consequences as a result of using the information within this book, whether or not this is in any way due to any negligent act. No guarantees of success are made. The author acknowledges that everyone's circumstances are different, everyone's past is different, everyone's fears are different, and the reader assumes responsibility if they choose to use any of the information contained herein. This book is general in nature and is provided for informational purposes only and is not warranted for content, accuracy or any other implied explicit purpose. This book does not provide professional advice and is not in any way recommended as individual advice. The reader should obtain their own independent advice. References to internet sites in this book shall not be construed to be an endorsement of the internet sites, the companies or organizations represented by the internet sites or of the information contained thereon, by the author, publisher or associated parties.

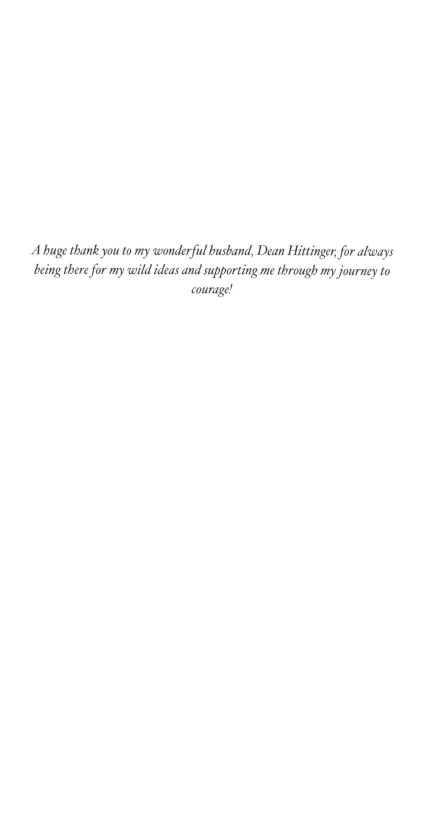

A huge thank you to my wonderful husband, Dean Hittinger, for always being there for my wild ideas and supporting me through my journey to courage!

PART 1 - THE START OF MY JOURNEY, THE FOUNDATION

Chapter One

WHAT HAPPENED TO MY COURAGE?

Was it an accident or did fear just creep up on you, or like me, was it both?

Have you ever had that feeling that you really were not supposed to do something and you did it anyway? Four of us had planned a great camping trip with our horses. It was the first time for all of us taking our four-legged partners up into the mountains outside of Los Angeles for a weekend getaway. We were going the weekend before Thanksgiving, so the weather would be cool and refreshing, and the mountains would be glorious. We had spent weeks conditioning our horses (and ourselves) for riding on the incredible mountain trails and getting to enjoy the scenery and cool, crisp air. It would be apple season, so we were looking forward to a great meal and some fresh deep-dish apple crisp for dessert after our long days in the saddle.

The weekend before our trip, there was a bad snowstorm right where we were planning on camping, and it was so bad, a few people lost their lives from hypothermia. That started my bad feeling about the trip, and I called my dad and sister and said I was concerned and maybe we should reconsider. They were convinced I was just having nerves about trying something new with the horses and all would be fine. The weather for our weekend was supposed to be absolutely perfect.

During the week, I packed up my truck and trailer, double

and triple checking my list. Since this was my first time for a camping trip with the horses, packing was not second nature. I just couldn't shake the feeling that somehow, this was going to be a mistake, but I kept preparing and getting ready, ignoring that feeling in my gut that something was going to go dreadfully wrong.

On that Friday morning, I went in to work as usual and tried to focus on the work at hand. At lunch time, the security guard came into the conference room to let me know that my truck was leaking diesel fuel in the parking lot. I rushed out to see that, sure enough, there was a pool of diesel under my truck. I took the rest of the afternoon off to see if the dealer could get it fixed in time for us to leave that afternoon.

Now, the feeling of dread was palpable. I can remember my sense of relief and the weight being lifted off my shoulders when the dealer said they would not have my truck fixed until Monday and they would give me a loaner car! Pure joy! I called my sister and let her know we would not be joining her for the weekend.

She wasn't having any of that and talked me into at least driving up in the dealer car and hanging out for the weekend. That seemed harmless, and I thought, "why not learn from them and then be better prepared next time?" So off I went to meet up at the campground. We decided to walk about the campground on the horses while my brother-in-law set up camp.

I got onto his horse (that I had never been on before) for a nice walk around the campground at sunset, and as soon as I touched the saddle, I knew something was drastically wrong. The 17-hand horse I was sitting on was standing on tippy toes and felt like a powder keg about to EXPLODE. The power and terror all wrapped up in those first 10 seconds made me realize I was in deep trouble.

I decided to get off as gently as I possibly could, petting him on the neck as I pulled my foot back out of the stirrup, and as soon as my foot was clear, HE RAN BACKWARDS about a hundred feet (or so it felt) until his feet caught on the edge of the road, and it catapulted him backwards on top of me and a split rail fence.

He was stuck upside down on top of me, rolled up against a tree, and he couldn't get off of me. I don't know how long we were stuck like that, but I knew it was the last I would ever see of this world; it seemed to be eternity.

They got him off of me and called 911, and thankfully, my brother-in-law, being a deputy sheriff, knew what to do until the ambulance arrived. I just knew I wasn't going to make it to the hospital; I was going to die right there in the ambulance.

God's hands were around me. I had only minor injuries and some crazy bruises from a bunch of pine cones. Physically, I was fine, but mentally, the TERROR WAS REAL and ingrained.

We found out the horse had been bitten by a Black Widow spider and thought I was trying to kill him. Talk about a random accident. This only escalated my fear since it could happen at any time, to any horse. It was an odd fear. I had no problem continuing to jump and ride in an arena but was terrified to ride on the trails, even the well-groomed trails by the stables where I kept my horse. I would break out into a sweat, hyperventilate, and really just could not mentally go on trail rides. As soon as a horse lifted its head, I jumped off, standing next to it, shaking while it looked at me quizzically, not understanding my feelings of terror.

Fast forward, almost 20 years later, my husband and I bought an amazing farm with trails on and off the property, and we even have access to ride down to a gorgeous lake. I realized that this fear was controlling my riding life and preventing me from finding my joy in the saddle! We even bought my husband a trail horse, so we could ride out together, but that wasn't happening.

I had to make the decision to trail ride again!

Chapter Two

FEARLESS KID, COURAGEOUS ADULT!

Leave your fear at the barn and enjoy riding your horse again!

I remember being that FEARLESS kid! I would ride the steep mountain trails in the early morning mist to watch the sunrise and then RACE home to shower and get to school. All summer, we would leave at 6 a.m. to ride miles to the river to swim all day in the blazing heat of summer, cool in the river and pools, and then race home before it got too dark to find our way.

We would play "Tag" in the lakes and ponds, swimming our horses and ponies in the cool water until they touched the bottom, and then we were "out" and had to go back out into the heat until everyone was done except the winner. Then, the game would start all over again. Our horses were FIT, and we were FIT from all the exercise.

We rode up steep little mountain trails that passed through tree groves and meadows. We would stop and have lunch, letting our ponies graze on the meadow grass while we enjoyed PB&J sandwiches. When we were done playing in the Angeles National Forest, we raced back down on the fire breaks, winner take all!

Then, when I turned 10, I was old enough to ride in the local mounted drill team, Blue Shadows. I learned a whole new level of riding and how to ride and drill with others. Most of us rode the local stable rental string horses, and I remember wanting Roach; he was my favorite. He was a tall, lean bay with a white star, and he was a challenge to ride, which I loved. I learned so much by riding different horses and having to do drills taking into account each horse's personality. I loved working with the other team members to ride to the best of our ability and make our team look great. The whole year, we prepared for the annual drill competition. It was amazing to see how much our riding improved and our horsemanship as well since that was part of the program.

When I turned fourteen, my mom took me with friends to watch a jumper show; that was the end of me playing around with horses, and I became a serious junior rider. I switched over 100% to the hunter/jumper/equitation world. We sold my child-hood horse and bought a junior hunter for me. My parents sold our house, and we moved to where I could easily ride to my lessons every day. I spent countless hours riding no irons and focused on my equitation and my skills at horsemanship. I groomed to pay for shows and mucked stalls to pay for lessons. I was in heaven as I worked my way through the ranks and had a blast doing the shows that I could afford.

I remember one year at the fall "Turkey" show in Santa Barbara how crowded the warm up ring was. It was CRAZY, with horses going every which way and jumping this way and that over the jumps. I remember thinking, "wow, this must have been what knights felt like, going in to battle." The one thing I don't remember about all those competitions was any fear; I know I had some, but those are not the memories I chose to keep. I remember the jumps, the floating dance over those fences with the horses, and the amazing friends on the show circuit.

I continued competing into adulthood and moved more into the jumper and equitation world. At this point, I became more of a passenger with grooms to take care of the horses and a trainer to improve the horses while I worked to pay for my passion.

I was still competing every other week, and it was my young horse I was just starting to compete on that I was planning on taking on that fateful camping trip.

After my accident, I wanted to find that FEARLESS child and live in her boots (or bare feet) again. It wasn't easy. There was not a lot of help out there. I talked to sports psychologists and other mental health professionals, but they really didn't understand the fact that a horse feels your energy and fear and reacts. With a horse, you can't "Fake it 'til you make it." They didn't know how to help me with the partnership with the horse being a factor.

I talked to, and worked with, a number of trainers, and they could help me with the horse, but they really didn't understand my fear; they didn't feel it and couldn't help me with my fear. Their answers were "just do it," or "you have to be the boss." There were bits and pieces that helped some but not enough for me to be at ease on trail rides.

I ended up on a journey to courage, a journey to health, and returning to that passion and joy I had as a child, living to ride!

Chapter Three

WHAT ARE THE KEYS TO COURAGE?

Keys unlock the secrets that have been stored inside of us, tramped down by that fear as it moves in and takes over.

When I realized I was terrified to go for a trail ride, something deep down inside of me snapped. It was like watching someone else and thinking, "no way would I ever be afraid to go for a nice relaxing trail ride," but it was me. I remember feeling so completely sad at not wanting to enjoy adventures on my horses and having let fear take over my joy of riding.

DECISION

One of the very first keys on my journey was I MADE THE DECISION to seek my courage. I had no idea where the journey would lead or what it would look like, but making the decision was a relief; it was the first step on the journey and the hardest step. It required commitment.

MIND & BODY

The second key was twofold, mind and body. Mindset has been a journey through my fear and finding bits of courage to hold on to and build on. I look back to my younger years and realize gaining courage is not much different for riding horses than for anything that you are afraid of - from speaking in public to heights to the dentist, in my case. Those are things I have found the courage to do. The biggest challenge with courage and horses is they don't let you "FAKE IT," and they will show you exactly what you are feeling, even if you are not admitting it. This was important for me. I realized I could look into the mirror of the horse and see my emotions clearly.

My body was easier to change once I figured stuff out. I remember when I was about five, wanting to sit on the floor and play a board game, but all my aunts and uncles declined, saying they could not sit on the floor with all their aches and pains. I was crushed and made a vow right then and there to not ever have to say no to sitting on the floor to play a game!

Fast forward into my fifties, and lo and behold, I was going to be challenged sitting on the floor to play with the grandkids. What I also realized was that the same reason I would not be able to sit on the floor was also impacting my riding. I would be sore and ache. I knew I wasn't communicating as clearly with my horses because I was stiff. There was nothing good about my health, and that had to change for me to get my confidence back.

KNOWLEDGE

The third key was knowledge. I knew I had it with the many years of riding. I knew how to ride. I knew how to communicate with the horses. I knew what to do in crazy situations, but this didn't help the fear. What this did help was the path to courage. Just as in doing anything that you are afraid of, if you have the knowledge, you can conquer the fear.

What areas could I improve in my knowledge?

The first thing was learning to communicate with the horse. Well, it was mostly learning how to listen. I was great at telling, as I had been taught for many years, but listening was a different matter altogether. How many times do we really "NOT" listen to the person talking to us, let alone our horses? I felt like I was discovering "Mr. Ed" in my horses, and boy, once I started listening, they could talk!

The second area of improvement was developing pre-ride checklists for myself and the horse. This gave me the confidence that yes, today was a good day to ride, or no, today was not a good day to ride. This could be because of either myself or my horse; we both had a say in the decision to go on an adventure.

The third area was gaining knowledge on basic fundamentals of riding and horsemanship. What building blocks did I need to put together so that I could build confidence while riding? What order did I need to follow with those blocks to get my courage back? The process of finding courage is no different than any other process. Being a Lean Six Sigma Engineer, (specialist in creating and streamlining business processes), you would have thought I had a process a long time before I got to the point of fear. But what if I had a process the day of my horse accident? Would I have gotten on? Would I have seen the stress on the horse while tacking up? Would I have noticed the horse wasn't right? The knowledge of the fundamentals provides the path to riding a horse confidently.

EXPERIENCE

The fourth key for me was experience. I had years of experience riding and competing, but I didn't have any experience overcoming fear. This was eye-opening for me. Just like the old adage of learning to ride a bike, learning to overcome fear is no different; you have to start, you can put on training wheels, and you can do lots of repetitions until you get it right. Eventually, you can remove the training wheels and just RIDE with courage again!

I had always thought, "I am an experienced rider, I can ride," but that accident showed me that there is a lot more to riding than having a groom hold the horse while you get on and go warm up and compete. I had only touched a small fraction of a relationship with a horse, even though I had spent 50 years with them.

I would require new tools to gain the experience I needed to overcome fear. It was like a scavenger hunt and one that I am happy to say I completed successfully! I have the building blocks and the tools to build my confidence back up to full-fledged COURAGE.

PART 2 - MIND AND BODY, RIDER AND HORSE

Chapter Four

WHAT DO FEAR AND COURAGE LOOK LIKE?

The Rattlesnake or the Branch? The Sword or the Shield?

Let's look at three scenarios and compare the similarities and the differences.

Scenario 1 – REAL FEAR:

Picture a beautiful sunny afternoon, riding along a trail with a gorgeous view, the rhythm of the horse's footfall on the trail is like a lullaby, instilling complete peace and joy. In the blink of any eye, you go from that place of deep peace to HIGH ALERT, blood pumping fast, heart racing, adrenaline rushing as you recognize a rattlesnake, lying a few feet ahead, sunning itself across the trail.

Scenario 2 – PERCEIVED FEAR:

Imagine a beautiful trail ride through the woods, light breeze blowing, keeping things cool. The horses are relaxed and just following along the winding trail around the trees, and the whole world looks magical. Then, you're suddenly brought to HIGH ALERT, heart racing, blood pounding in your ears, palms sweaty and adrenaline coursing through your body, as you recognize a stick lying across the trail that looks exactly like a snake.

Scenario 3 – IMAGINARY FEAR:

It's a gorgeous day, riding through the edge of field with the light and shadows playing in the grasses. Your mind wanders to an accident you had a few years ago when you came across a snake in the edge of the woods, and you start to get nervous; your breathing rate increases and becomes shallow. You start to tense your body, and your heart rate increases. You are not sure you can go on; you want to just go back or get off. The memory was from years ago; the fear is today.

Let's look at similarities first. In all three, your horse FELT your FEAR. This is so important to realize and understand. Your horse doesn't know whether your fear is real, perceived, or imaginary; it is a prey animal, and its life depends on feeling the fear of the herd around it. Imagine if you are sitting in a room and a person in the hallway yells, "FIRE!" You have no idea if it is a real fire, if there is just smoke and it is perceived fire, or if the person is completely wrong and there isn't anything. You will take ACTION. Your horse will also take ACTION.

In all three, you felt FEAR. Your body has no idea if the fear is real, perceived, or imaginary; it will prepare for ACTION. Your bodily responses are in full swing as a result of the fear in your mind. Your body will release adrenaline and prepare for the situation, no matter which type of fear you are feeling.

Now, what are the differences?

The first thing that stands out to me is that scenario 1 is the only one in which ACTION is valuable. The other two have no value in taking action. If you have ever seen a herd in a field, this is true. If there is something to be afraid of, they all run. If it is a false alarm, they all go back to grazing. There is no value in taking action unless there is real fear.

The second thing that stands out for me is that the first two scenarios are a beautiful ride, there is a blip, and then the beautiful ride can continue on, just as a herd would do, either with taking action or with knowing there is no action to take.

But the third scenario requires intervention to really enjoy riding. It will suck the joy out of a ride, and it will fill it with all the "what if something goes wrong" thoughts. Your mind will go down the rabbit hole unless you change its course and do something to stop that imaginary fear from ruining your ride.

We will focus on scenario 3; let's get back to the JOY of riding and the search for the "what if things go right" thoughts. This may seem impossible at first, but with practice, you will become a master at getting your mind back on track. As soon as you recognize that fear is imaginary, here is the plan:

- Recognize the imaginary fear
- Laugh at the power of our imagination (you can't be afraid and laugh at the same time)
- Breathe into your present moment
- Picture your VISION (we will talk about this in a later chapter)
- See your surroundings
- Feel the rhythm of the horse

The great news is that just small changes, small shifts in thought, can have HUGE impacts on courage, and that courage brings huge amounts of JOY. We will talk about those changes on our journey through the following chapters:

Health
Vision
Communication
Courage Pennies
Ground Play
Pre-Ride
Relaxation
Arena Play
Adventures

Chapter Five

HAPPY HEALTHY HORSE AND HAPPY HEALTHY RIDER

How much does health play a role in our courage and confidence?

Toxins

I have three amazing, quiet mares who are best friends. They get along, are rarely in season, and if they are in season, it is short and a non-issue. I, on the other hand, used to have horrendous hot flashes, standing in line at the store and almost passing out type hot flashes, ten to twenty an hour. I figured it out and stopped the hot flashes, for good.

It was a very harmonious farm, until one day, when I found SIX jars of a popular fly control ointment. I had the thought, "wow, I need to use these up before they go bad."

It was all good, and we were all happy for about 24 hours. Then, along came a few hot flashes, out of the blue after not having any for over a year. I continued putting the fly stuff on the horses' bellies and ears. About 48 hours later, I was having really bad hot flashes, every hour, feeling yucky, and I happened to notice that my three lovely mares were starting to get angry with each other.

By the third day, I felt horrible, and the three girls looked like they were ready for a bar room brawl - ears pinned, kicking at each other, all in season, and just in general, our farm has gone to hell in a hand basket!

Let me just say, even if I felt like riding, I would not have gotten on those girls. It would not have been safe! It dawned on me that the cause of my hot flashes and the cause of the mare brawl was the fly ointment! How much of the bad rap mares get is caused by chemicals we are using on those mares? As soon as I stopped the ointment, we all went back to our happy place.

If you are having challenges with your horses, observe the things you are using on your horses and ask some questions about the ingredients.

Physical

Physical is twofold, rider and horse. As I mentioned earlier, when I hit my fifties, I could feel the gremlins creeping in and taking over my body. It didn't happen overnight; it was more like watching water boil, slowly. I realized I had trouble putting on my socks, getting out of bed in the mornings, and I had added creaks and groans, sounding like a creaky old house. I knew I would not be able to sit on the floor and play board games with the grandkids comfortably and that I had let down my five-year-old self. I made the decision to change all that.

The main things I changed were eliminating processed cane sugar and wheat flour of any kind. There was other stuff too, but this was the main change. It was very quick; I noticed I felt better than I had in a long time. After a year of this, I felt as good as I did as a kid. The best thing about it was my riding felt great! I rode in a three-day clinic after not riding much for six months, and for the first time in my life, I was NOT sore. What we put in our bodies can have huge consequences.

From a horse's perspective, pain can do a number on your confidence and your horse's confidence in you! I purchased a nice 3-year-old off the track, Taika, and, in the first three months, discovered she had fractured her skull at the track flipping in the starting gate, and that was probably caused by the kissing spine that we found, a condition in which the horse's vertebrae rub together. I didn't feel like I had a lot of choices, and my friends and the vets all strongly recommended letting her go graze in heaven. I just couldn't do that until I had exhausted all options. I found an equine chiropractor to work with me to bring her back to health, and it was an amazing three-year journey to health for her and tremendous learning for me.

Our horses cannot speak in words, but they speak in so many other ways – a limp here, a little bit of swelling there. They may not move forward easily with soft feet and mind. Pain can be small or it can be huge. It can be an electric shock that lasts for only seconds, like with kissing spine, or chronic pain that they have just learned to live with. In all cases, we should know our horses, their condition, their health, and their pain.

Nutrition

This is one of my favorite "hidden" ways to look at our relationship with our horses and our FEAR triggers. I was at a show with one of my hunters, and on the second day, I pulled her out of the stall, and she was just on edge. I couldn't get her to focus to tack her up; she was best described as having "ants in her pants"! She was dancing around, and I felt like I had a fire-breathing dragon on the end of the lead rope. I was able to get one of the teenage riders to jump on her and canter the warm up arena for forty-five minutes until she finally settled, but this was just not like her, and so I investigated. Well, it turned out, she was given three flakes of alfalfa instead of grass hay for breakfast! It was like giving a child three pounds of candy and then wanting them to sit still. It isn't going to happen.

If your horse's nutrition is not matched to the horse and the exercise levels, it is going to cause problems. If the problems don't show up in having a horse flying at the end of a lead rope or jigging or, worse yet, bolting on a trail ride, they will show up in the horse's health - laminitis being one of the worst things I can think of. I do not feed any grain and no soy either. I feed bare minimum of anything except 24/7 good quality hay and 24/7 pasture. I feed vitamins and minerals that coordinate with the hay in my area, so they don't have a deficiency (or excess). I feed chia seeds for gut health, and I feed raspberry leaves for mares so they are not "mare-ish." I will add a few things here and there as needed for specific health reasons, but keep it simple; it doesn't need to be complex and expensive.

For me, the other half of this partnership, nutrition has been a journey in itself, and there are a few things I have found that work for me. I used to have those afternoon slumps at horse shows, but then I found my "red drink" which is very yummy and gives me an amazing feeling, (see recipe in www.elisehit-tinger.com/page/book-bonus)! This is a high antioxidant drink that I can make up the night before a show. I put it in the fridge and just take it with me for when I start feeling a slump coming on.

I have adjusted my vitamins and minerals to my food intake for optimal health, and I have to say, I feel great. On the days that I am not away at shows, I mix up a smoothie with my red drink and throw in lots of fresh ingredients. If you are interested, you can contact me through my website at elisehittinger.-com, and I can get you specific information.

Chapter Six

MY PERFECT RIDE

The future looks like what you dream about today!

Vision

I had to create the vision of what I want my ride to look like. It seemed simple, but my first try looked like a stick figure. I had to laugh; it reminded me of when I was a kid and playing hangman with my sister. It was so bleak and didn't have any life to it. Guess what? The results I was getting from that vision were flat, minor, and not much different than where I was.

To create a really good vision, I had to practice and learn, a little like riding a horse. I had to work the muscles of creating a vision to make it AMAZING. I heard once, "I am the painter of my destiny," and that really is what we are doing with setting a vision.

Grab a piece of paper, notebook, or journal and do this along with me. See if you can create the ultimate ride for you.

I started with location. I want to ride from my house to the lake that is by our farm. Location, I like to think of as setting the scene. The first part is a dirt road down the hillside to the creek, and then following the creek along the bottom to the lake. This is what I mean by "stick figure." It is so bare, and there isn't any really inspiration to it. So let's build on.

Next, let's add some visual details to our vision. The sun was shining through the trees and making the trail light up like a magical garden. The moss on the sides of the trail is an amazing deep green in contrast to the rich browns of the trees. The fall leaves are covering the trail like a carpet of reds, oranges, and browns. The sunshine reflecting off the lake in the distance looks like a field of diamonds playing in the light. Do you see how adding visual details improves the vision and gives it some life?

Let's take it a little further and see how many senses we can add to really "FEEL" this ride.

The day of the ride is warm with the sun shining and a light breeze. Running my hands through the soft fur of my horse while I am grooming and tacking up reminds me of the stuffed animals I cuddled up with as a child. I can hear the deep breathing, the munching of the hay, the swishing of my horse's tail as we get ready to go on our adventure, and it brings an overall feeling of peace.

As I mount up, I have an overwhelming feeling that all is right with the world. The birds are singing in the distance, and it is music to my ears. As we start off down the trail, I can hear the light rustling of the leaves in the trees, and they shimmer in the sunlight like sequins on my favorite New Year's Eve dress. The fresh smell of earth after the gentle rain we had last night has me feeling the connection to Mother Earth.

The rhythmical footfalls of my horse, brushing through the leaves as she ambles down the moss laden trail sounds like a lullaby and brings that feeling of wellbeing. The reins in my hands are like holding hands with my best friend; they are communication without words.

So now, we have added in hearing, smell, touch, feelings, and sight. The more detail you can put into your vision, the more it will come to life. The ultimate goal, for any vision, is to be able to FEEL IT, in every cell of your body, like it is a memory of something that has already happened. Your brain will not know that it hasn't already happened. By immersing yourself in the vision, it will bring it to reality.

One of my favorite vision stories happened when I was watching this AMAZING jumper that was WAY out of my price range, and I just grabbed a notebook and wrote all about him as if he was mine. I didn't even think about it again. That notebook disappeared and was out of my mind. Three years later, that jumper became mine. That was the most fun nine years I have ever had on a horse, and I know, without a doubt, putting my vision in great detail down on paper created my future with him.

If you are going to make up stuff about your ride that is coming up, why not make up an amazing ride? What does your vision look like? Don't rush through this; take your time.

The steps to creating an amazing vision:

- Set the location - think of movies and how they set up the scene with the location.
- Add the visual details. Add in all the sights you can think of on your amazing ride.
- Add in the touch and feel of your ride, from feeling the fur on the neck of your horse to the touch of the breeze on your cheek.
- What sounds are you hearing? The rustling of leaves under the horse's feet? Birds singing? The rhythm of the horse's footfalls?
- Finally, add in all your emotions. Your feelings as you go for this ride are the most important part of the vision and will set the vision into your mind.

PART 3 - KNOWLEDGE IS POWERFUL

Chapter Seven

DID YOU SAY "MR. ED"?

Having a conversation with your horse is important!

I remember as a kid watching Mr. Ed and thinking how normal conversations with horses would be. Of course, they can talk to you. Of course, you listen to them. I grew up riding and enjoying horses in my life, but over time, I forgot how to listen to the horses. I forgot how to have conversations with my best four-legged friends. There were so many other horse people in my life that didn't listen to horses, and they taught me how to not listen to my horses as well.

The journey to two-way communication started with a horse that refused to let me continue not listening to her. I remember the day I woke up to what she was telling me. I used to go out in the pasture to "catch" Taika and bring her in. Some days, I didn't have any problem, and some days, she just stayed two feet ahead of me. This went on for months, if not years, before I had the epiphany; the days I couldn't catch her, I was not present, not in the moment, and not listening. This was when I really started my search for "Mr. Ed," or to be more accurate, my quest to be more like Wilbur.

What Taika was showing me was if I was present, in the moment when I went to be with her, she would come to me and put her head in the halter. I had to have the halter ready, the lead rope organized, and I had to just be there with her, in that moment.

If, on the other hand, I was thinking about work, or financial issues, or anything else that we get our minds going on, I could NOT catch her. She would just stay two feet in front of me, and this could last from minutes to hours. When I finally would get present and in the moment, she would allow me to put the halter on, but she was GRUMPY. She let me know that coming to spend time with her meant just that, and if she had to remind me, I was in the doghouse.

This was my wakeup call. There was a different way to be present with my horses. I could listen to them. They had something to say. I am by no means perfect at this; it is a process. Sometimes, they say very loudly "NO," and I have to do it anyway for health or safety reasons. But for the most part, I try and listen. What I have noticed is the more I listen, the more they share with me.

I look for subtle things in their communication. When watching the herd, they usually give very subtle cues to each other before things go sideways if the other one doesn't listen. This is especially easy to see at feeding time. Binky is my lead mare and can be very aggressive. She will have her face in her food bowl, and Michelle or Taika will walk up with their head sideways, looking like they are asking if they can share. Sometimes, she will let them put their heads in the bucket. I can tell she is going to because her ears go back, but not completely back. Sometimes, she is going to bite, and I can tell that, too. They come up asking, and before they get within 5 feet of the bucket, her ears pin, and if they keep coming, she will charge with teeth bared and bite.

How many times do we not notice the subtle clues, the head sideways, the ears a little off, the tail swish, the not wanting to pick up a foot, and so on? Horses are always talking to us; we can always be better at listening. The better we get at listening, the more courage we will have, and the more we will be rewarded with our relationship with our horses!

Chapter Eight

CONCEPT OF COURAGE PENNIES

Once the decision is made, mountains will move.

Courage pennies are those moments of courage that you feel and add to your courage piggy bank. The more courage you feel, the more courage you "will" feel. Think about something difficult that you learned and, in the end, it was easy. The same thing goes with learning courage. Collect those courage pennies!

Rider

I have to admit, I was petrified of the dentist since I was little, to the point of passing out in the waiting room. This is a completely irrational fear, one we call imaginary fear. I think all of us have some level of fear about something that is imaginary. Public speaking? Heights? Spiders? Snakes?

So why not learn how to get anxious and then relax? Practice it. Use tools to help. When I decided to change my health, I found a natural product, Stress Away, that really has made a difference for me in being able to get stressed and then relax. (If you are interested in finding out more, see the Anchoring with Aroma section on my website http://elisehittinger.com/page/book-bonus). I have to say, my last trip to the dentist, I fell asleep in the chair getting my teeth cleaned! This for me was

HUGE! So many times, we think about getting our horses relaxed, but we forget to practice getting ourselves relaxed.

It is important to practice this when you are not with your horse, and then, you have that tool when you are with your horse. There are a number of ways of doing this, but so far, the Stress Away has worked brilliantly for me.

Process:

1. Close my eyes and think about the dentist
2. Let myself get in that anxious state
3. Breathe deeply in a square (From Mindsets Matter, see link on www.elisehittinger.com/page/book-bonus)
4. count 4 out
5. hold for 4
6. count 4 in
7. hold for 4
8. Repeat until I am nice and calm.
9. When I feel that calm wash over me, I SMELL the Stress Away deeply! I let that smell flood over my calm state.
10. Repeat all the steps until as soon as you smell Stress Away, you feel immense calm.

At first, I did this at home, just closing my eyes and thinking about the dentist office. Then, I worked up to the waiting room and then the actual chair. It worked for me. Lots of courage pennies were gained here!

Horse

With the horse, it is a little more challenging since you are influencing another being. There are a few things that are important to think about with the horse. The first thing is to only change one thing at a time to work on relaxation. My journey with Michelle to a clinic this past summer is a great example of this.

I knew I was taking Michelle to a three-day clinic, and I wanted to make sure we were as prepared as possible for a successful trip. I started with riding her at home. Then, I added riding her around my other two horses, so she got used to multiple horses. Next, I loaded her and unloaded her from the trailer many times. She was a racehorse so is a great hauler, but I wanted her used to my trailer since I was planning on hauling in each day.

The day of the clinic, I hauled her in, led her up to the arena, and mounted by climbing on the fence. The only thing new for her was a new place; I had done all the rest before. We played for about three hours that first day with the clinic exercises.

I ended up letting her stay the night since they had a nice corral for her, and she seemed really happy and relaxed there. Day two, I got on at the trailer and rode with the other horses up to the clinic area. Then, we did day two of the clinic. This was all very successful, and we didn't overwhelm her at all. The only time she got rattled was when I was leading her around after a bath and a crop duster helicopter started flying crazy loops right above us. The clinician rode down to us and led her back up to where she had been for the clinic, so she was again in familiar surroundings, and she calmed right down.

Courage pennies add up really fast when focusing on "change only one thing at a time." You gain courage pennies, and your horses gain courage pennies too!

Another great thing to do with your horse is to get them "UP," then get them to relax, and then get them "UP" and then relaxed and help them also learn to practice this. It is a little bit like desensitizing but different. I love to use a water bottle or plastic bag.

Get the horse walking around you; the key here is for the feet to be moving. Crinkle the bottle. Most horses will react and get scared; let them keep moving their feet and keep crinkling the bottle until they relax. Don't do it any harder or softer. It is important to keep the crinkling sound the same until they relax. This teaches them that when they get "UP," they can find their own relaxation. I did this so much with Taika that when I crinkle a bottle now, she stops, faces me, cocks a hind foot, and completely relaxes. I have also seen it done with walking away from them with the bottle crinkling.

This builds up courage pennies for you and your horse as well.

Chapter Nine

GROUND PLAY

Foundation is built one brick at a time, or in our case, one step at a time.

Did you ever play with a kaleidoscope as a child? It was one of my cherished toys. I loved being able to look in the tube and see how many colors I could count and how many shapes, and how many lines and just really immersing myself into the design. It was a way to practice observation. I look at ground play with the horses the same way.

Observation makes ground play so much more valuable. I can fine tune my timing. I can see when I communicate clearly or when I get things muddled. I can see when I listen to what my horse is telling me, and I can see when I am not listening. If the horse is relaxed and playing with me in line with my picture in my head, we are having a great conversation.

If, on the other hand, my horse's head is raised, their breathing is getting faster, and the tension in their body is increasing, I know we are not having a conversation. I am either telling the horse what to do and they are not understanding, or they are trying to tell me something and I am not listening. Either way, the observation is knowledge, and the more I practice this, the better my riding communication will be later on.

Playing over poles on the ground, I can move one foot or move two feet, but choosing ahead of time and then executing really shows me visually how my timing is, where I can improve, and how to better ask for the movement the next time. If I ask the horse to back six steps, and they back seven or eight, I asked too hard and didn't release at the right time. If I plan to have my horse move its hind end away from me for three steps, crossing under, and they move two, I released too soon, or if they cross behind, I am not at the right angle.

Observation while doing ground play does a few things:

1. It improves your timing through your focus.
2. You are "IN" the moment, you are all in.
3. You have a plan and execute the plan.
4. The more you do little exact things with your horse, the better your connection will be with your horse.
5. The more you play with your horse, the better you become at listening and having a conversation.
6. The more you observe your horse, the earlier you catch potential health issues, a slight limp, a stiff side, not stretching the leg under.
7. It builds your courage. Every time you can ask your horse for something and execute it, you build your courage with that horse, putting courage pennies in your courage bank.
8. You can express your creativity. Think of things to do on the ground with your horse that are challenging and fun.

We talked a little about this, but all of this really improves the connection with your horse. They become better at listening to you, and you become better at listening to them. It improves the two-way communication we talked about earlier.

The outcomes of ground play are a horse that understands what you are asking and how you ask. You learn how to ask that horse and how to help that horse learn new things. All of this builds confidence for you and for the horse! Put some more courage pennies into your courage bank.

Here are some exercises that I LOVE:

1. One thing I love to do is get them really good at handling their feet, to the point I can write their initials with their toes in the dirt with all four feet. I add challenge to this by standing next to the horse's right side, picking up the left foot, front or hind, and writing their initials. I also stand on the left side and repeat with the right-side feet.

2. Obstacle courses are a very good way to really get to know your horse. Even if you don't have an official course, find things (that are safe) and play with them. I had a piece of plywood that I taught Taika to stand on when I gave her a cue. I put that piece of plywood up on top of the cavalettis to store it, and one day, I accidently gave the cue while I was talking to someone else, and Taika went over and put her front feet up on the cavalettis. It was so cute and rewarding!

3. Pick things to step over or around and practice moving one foot. Then move that foot back. This also is really good for trailer loading.

4. Ground tying. This is one of the first things I ground play with. I get them to stand while I do other stuff, but I get them to stay focused on me. If they start to look away, I will move something or do something to bring their attention back. I make this more challenging by adding cues from a distance. If I wiggle my fingers toward them, I want them to take one step back or one step forward. I hold my hand up like a stop sign for "stand."

5. Setting jumps. I love to have them help me set jumps. When I am carrying a pole, I get them to put their nose on it and walk with me. That way, I really don't have to watch them while I am setting jumps; they play with me.

6. I love playing at liberty. When Taika was rehabilitating from kissing spine, I lunged her at liberty for almost three years to build her abs. We got to where I could lunge her almost anywhere, at liberty, and have her circle closer to me or further out just from my thoughts. It was mostly at the walk and canter since that is what builds the abs the most, so I started this at the walk, but eventually, we got really good even at the canter at liberty. I could have her change directions, slow the canter, speed up the canter. It was a glorious feeling; that connection was at a heart level.

These are just a few examples; you can get as creative as you want and have as much fun as you want. Once your horse understands that you are playing with them, they usually get really into the playing.

PART 4 – EXPERIENCE TIME, SADDLE UP AND GO

Chapter Ten

PRE-RIDE CHECKLISTS

Would you fly on a plane that had not been checked? Would you fly with a pilot that wasn't mentally ready?

I am so excited to be sharing with you the pre-ride checklists. These are the most important part of riding horses, in my opinion; the rest will work itself out, but this is the golden key!

Pre-Ride Checklist for the <u>RIDER</u>!

- Set your vision on the way to the barn. Remember that amazing vision we created in the previous chapter? Put yourself into that vision, breathe into it, be in that vision, feel that vision take a hold of you. Know that your vision is coming true. There are a few things this will do for you. First of all, it pushes the fear out and doesn't leave any room for it; you are filled up with the peace of your vision. Secondly, all the "other" stuff falls away when you are focused on your vision. You can't be picturing an amazing ride and also be thinking about what you are cooking for dinner; it's one or the other, so choose to think about your vision.
- Be present while grooming your horse. Really connect

with your horse; be in the moment. Notice how calm and quiet your horse is and if there are any holes in the responses to you. Be present in the grooming process and see what your horse enjoys and maybe what he doesn't enjoy as much. Practice the feet connection while you clean the feet.

- Find things to laugh at while grooming and tacking up. It is impossible to feel fear while you are laughing with your horse. Does he give you a funny look; can you see the cartoon bubble above his head telling you that you are taking too long? Picture as many funny things as you can, and that, too, will fill you up with joy.

- This is my favorite part. I use "anchors" for calm and for courage. This can really be anything, but the idea is to feel that sense of calm and then anchor it to something. For me, I use smell. I use Stress Away (like I described in the dentist challenge). I put on a lava bead bracelet and put a drop of Stress Away on my right wrist. That way, if I feel my nerves starting to come up, I can smell the Stress Away, and it has been anchored to calm. The second anchor I have is for leadership. I use a lava bead bracelet on my left wrist, with Thieves essential oil blend, and I have anchored leadership to the smell of Thieves. This gives me the courage to lead when my horse is unsure. (For more information on how to do the anchoring, see www. elisehittinger.com/page/book-bonus section on Anchoring with Aroma)

Pre-Ride Checklist for the <u>HORSE</u>!

There is a lot of information out there for this, so I am going to share one of my stories. The other day, I had an appointment with the equine chiropractor; he comes once a month to adjust my girls. That day, it was really windy when we got up, but the horses seemed fine and ate breakfast without issue. I went out about an hour before the appointment; I like to make sure they are warmed up and ready for their adjustment, and I like to observe them, like I talk about in the ground play chapter, to see if I can tell what needs adjustment.

I pulled Binky out first, and it was very apparent that something was going on. It is windy here quite often, so I really didn't think much about it, but it was like flying a horse kite. She was at the end of the lead rope in the air above me, over and over. I did my usual things to refocus her on me, but she wasn't having any of that.

I decided to put Binky back and try Taika, who is the laziest horse I have ever owned. She will stand and watch the horses playing and running and not put forth the effort to even move out of their way. As I pulled Taika out of the pasture, there was a sense of electricity around her that I could feel. Horse number two was also pretending to be a kite. I really wasn't sure what was going on, but I knew it was something extraordinary. They are almost never like this.

Just as I was going to put her away and call the chiropractor to cancel, he pulled in. We decided to try and adjust Taika since she was off in her left hind, but it was absolutely dangerous.

If this had been a day I was planning on riding, there were so many clues that I would have gone through, and I would have known not to get on. They didn't eat dinner until after 9 p.m. that night. I had fed at 5 p.m., so I knew that something was still going on. The next day, they were still unsettled and had trouble focusing on breakfast, so my husband and I went on a search. We found a dead turkey in the far side of the horse pasture. I have no idea what had killed it, but I am sure this was what had the horses upset for almost 24 hours.

If it had been a riding day, I could have pushed through and ridden, but that would have, most likely, ended in a disaster. This was a dramatic situation but still shows a lot of the things I look for, just on a larger scale.

Here is my pre-ride checklist for the horse:

1. Does the horse come to me and put its head in the halter? In the case I just mentioned, they were not focused on me, and I had to put the halter on them.
2. Does the horse come with me or do I have to lead it? The example I gave was an extreme case, but what if it was more subtle such as they were not walking right beside me and not excited to go on an adventure? I would definitely check it out and make sure they were good.
3. Is there a change in the horse from normal? If the horse is normally quiet, as my three are, and all of a sudden, they are nervous or spooky, that would be a change. If they are normally forward and excited, are they quiet and lethargic? Look for differences from their normal.
4. Do I notice anything unusual while grooming and tacking up? Do they flinch at any spot grooming? Do they start to pin ears or move away from me while grooming? Do they paw while grooming? Is it hard to pick up a foot? Grooming is a great time to really check out the horse's mood and focus.
5. Has the horse been eating, and if not, have I given them a bunch of hay to fill them up while I groom and tack up? A horse's acid splashes up and can cause discomfort if their belly isn't full while riding, the exact opposite of humans.

These are my pre-ride lists, but they are in no way comprehensive. Really think about what you do when prepping you and your horse and consciously make it a routine. Practice going through the list for you and for your horse.

Chapter Eleven

RELAXED MOUNTING

To climb up on a 1300-pound soul and ride with the wind is the best gift a person can ever receive.

With your amazing vision in your head, being fully present with your horse, and having your horse fully present with you, it is time to start your journey as one. I think of the mounting block as the runway for take-off in an airplane. It is the last chance to identify any problems that should be addressed before getting on, and it is the launching pad for your journey.

I like to do a lot of mounting and dismounting from all kinds of objects. I am way too short to mount from the ground now that I have "aged" a little. I have to get creative, and my horses have to understand that. What I have found is that the more things I can climb up onto and have them walk up to so I can climb back off of them, the better our partnership becomes, and the safer I am during mounting and dismounting.

I think my favorite mounting story was with Michelle. I took her to a clinic after only riding her a few times. I got to the clinic late since I took my time loading her, and it took longer than I had allotted. I unloaded her, tacked her up, and led her to the clinic area a few hundred yards away. She was perfect for the walk up, and they had a round pen set up for me since this was one of my first rides on her and the very first ride off property. I did a tiny bit of ground play with her, and she was so quiet, I knew I would be fine. I climbed up the round pen fence and got on. This was the first time I had even considered getting on with anything other than a mounting block. She was perfect and moved in closer to the fence to make it easier for me. I was so proud of her. Racehorses are taught to walk while the jockey mounts, so to me, this was a huge step in Michelle's training and in her overall demeanor.

Because Michelle is so young, I would do 30 minutes or so and then either get off on the fence or just get off in the pen, and I repeated this four or five times in each session. She was perfect. On the second day of the clinic, I wanted to ride up with the other participants, so I led her to a 3-foot tall tree stump next to the trailer and got on. She never moved until I asked her to walk off. It was so rewarding and a great way to build my confidence with her. We rode up to the clinic area with two of the other clinicians, crossing through a cemetery and across a road with no issues.

I think my best mounting in a potentially bad situation was with Taika. I brought her up to the mounting block on a some-what cloudy and slightly windy day, and she was so quiet and just standing at the mounting block. I had completed the pre-ride checklists for both of us, so I was fairly confident it would be a great ride.

I had decided to get on from the right side on a whim, which I don't do very often because it is 40 years of habit getting on the left and hard for me to change. Just as I was swinging my left leg over her butt, the cat caught a young rabbit that had been hiding under the mounting block. This happened right under Taika's belly! She was shocked, I was shocked, but she was so good and just picked her feet up in place, trying to keep from stepping on the cat and its friend while I finished mounting and got my wits about me.

I asked her to move off, and we had the best ride I have ever had. She is normally really lazy, but this day, she was FLOAT-ING; it was an amazing ride! And that cat played with that rabbit for almost the entire ride, in and out of the arena, back and forth all around us in the bushes just outside the arena.

The key with mounting is that it is the final check to make sure that everything is good. I knew from all the pre-ride work I had done that Taika was good for the ride. I knew that I was in the right frame of mind. Even a cat and a rabbit could not interfere with that amazing memorable mounting and ride.

Chapter Twelve

PLAY IN THE ARENA

Fast, faster, fastest – get comfortable with speed!

Get comfortable with speed in the arena before heading out on the trails. This was one of the first things I learned when I first started playing in an arena. I think I was 11 or 12 years old. I decided to take my horse to our very first gymkhana and really had no idea what I was doing. I watched a few other riders first in the pole bending and thought, "wow, I can do this." We walked into the arena, and I realized that I had no clue how to go about executing what everyone else made look so easy. I did the first round starting out at a trot and then heard my family cheering me on, so I started to lope, and by the end of the night, I was galloping! I didn't win any awards that night, but I learned what I could do if I made up my mind to do it.

I was way out of my comfort zone, but I did it anyway. My horse and I both had a really good time. The best part was I then knew that I could go fast and love it. We had a great area where I could really open up and gallop on the trails. I felt like a young cowgirl, out on the range, looking for lost cattle.

About that time, I discovered and joined a mounted drill team. This was one of the highlights of my riding as a kid. I remember those cool Friday evenings, waiting in line to pick a horse from the rental string. Riding different horses every week was a great learning experience.

Drill team was all about coordination, not only with other riders, but with horses of different personalities as well. We would ride at the walk, trot, and canter. We would do "wheels" with sixteen of us all in a row, the inside ones walking and the outside riders cantering. We would do split wheels with eight facing one way and eight facing the opposite way and we would execute a circle. Talk about a way to get comfortable and build confidence!

That confidence carried over to showing hunters and riding in the equitation divisions. I gained skills in guiding a horse through the corners of the arena to set up the line of the jumps. I learned how to adjust the stride of the horse to make the jumps seem effortless. I improved my riding through exercises of balance and connection with the horses. I continue in the jumpers and equitation even now, forty years later, and I still love these disciplines of riding.

The play in the arena is so important. It lets you freely connect with your horse in a more controlled environment than out on trails. It allows you to get comfortable with balance and movement of the horse and yourself without worrying about trees jumping in front of you or creeks showing up when you least expect them. The arena is a place to hone your skills as a rider in preparation for great adventures out in the wild, wild, west.

The crazy thing for me was I have no problem jumping over fences and competing in jump offs, but going out on the trail is where I had to overcome my fear. Knowing that I could ride made that so much easier.

Some of my favorite arena play exercises:

1. Poles! I love everything about using poles on the ground, either random poles or patterns. Poles are as much for me as they are for the horse. The benefits

for me are focus and a way to see incremental change.
I can pick a pole and walk to it, asking the horse to
walk with purpose. Then, I can pick another pole and
ask for a nice trot and then move up to right lead
canter and left lead canter. It is a set distance, and it
gives a definite end point. Poles are also so good for
the horse with picking up their feet, helping warm up
their back, and helping them to figure out "lifting"
through their abs. You can think of this as ten courage
pennies.

2. Playing with circles. I love to play with circles and
combinations of circles. I like to see how round I can
make them, and if I can put four together, just
touching my tracks to make a four-leaf clover pattern.
Can I start on a large circle and spiral my horse into a
small circle and then spiral back out to the large circle
again? I like to do circles with the bend to the inside
and with the bend toward the outside. I would give
these twenty courage pennies.

3. Obstacles are a blast. They can be as simple as tarps
and pieces of plywood. They don't have to be
complex. Pool noodles and umbrellas are great for
playing with on and off the horse. I do a lot of taking
my sweatshirt off and putting it back on (zipper ones
only, so my helmet always stays on.) Empty water
bottles and plastic bags are great too. If you think,
"oh, I could never do that," then that is a great
opportunity to do it. You can do it in the ground play
first and then incorporate it into riding. The
interesting thing is if you think it is scary, so will your
horse; they take their cue from you. I love banging on
things as I ride past them. It's not quite as much fun
as the wild west and shooting off a horse, but I think
that would be fun too! Thirty courage pennies for
playing with obstacles.

4. Soccer! Get one of those great big balls and play with the horse pushing it. I have found the key to this one is to look where you are going and not to look at the ball. If you combine the ball and the poles, it is a great way to learn finesse in communication. You can practice guiding your horse with just your legs and see if you can move the ball to different poles on the ground. It is just really fun! Playing with the soccer ball is worth 50 courage pennies.

5. If you have other people you can play with, Simon Says, Red Rover, and Tag are all games that I love to play with others. This is also great for getting ready to trail ride with others. Games with others would also be worth 50 courage pennies.

This is all good practice for things that might come up on the trail and really helps you and your horse understand each other. These are also good ways to find any remaining holes in either your riding or in the communication between your horse and you. Remember as you go through these exercises to mentally put your courage pennies into your courage bank!

Chapter Thirteen

GO ON ADVENTURES!

Being with my horse frees my soul!

So how do you go from feeling safe on the ground and riding in the arena to going on adventures? Here are the tools I have put into my toolbox that have helped me tremendously.

Four Steps

When I started going on adventures again, I was still working on my courage, so I started where I could. The most important thing was to start. I am embarrassed to say that my first few rides were based on FOUR steps. I would take four steps, stop, re-evaluate how I felt, pause, breathe. If I felt comfortable, I would reward myself with one courage penny, and I would take four more steps. Those first few rides, I made it 50 feet. This was HUGE for me, and it seems so crazy now that I was thrilled with 50 feet. It was a rush, and it felt great. I encourage you to find that comfort zone and start.

Video Game

Once I got good with four steps, I went to the video game mentality (thank you to Warwick Schiller). I like to play Wii Fit, and the obstacle course is my favorite. I think of it like a trail ride. When I would not make it on an obstacle, I would go back to the beginning and repeat all the steps. This was HUGE for me when I thought about trail riding again. What are the benefits of this?

1. You get to practice each thing, over and over and over, each time making it better and better. The first time I did the obstacle course on Wii, I didn't make it through the first obstacle. I had to practice it and get better each time and then progress to the next obstacle. When I finally made it to the end, I celebrated! I knew at a cellular level how to do the obstacle course. I had muscle memory; I could duplicate it. Do the same thing with your horse.

2. I like to think of my rides in stages. Let's pick 200 feet as the first "obstacle" in our riding game. In that 200 feet, ask the horse to bend left, bend right, halt, back five steps, and do a small circle each direction. If, at any point, the horse or you are not together and it doesn't feel right, return to the starting point and start the pattern over.

3. You and your horse grow together, get better together, and become a partnership. You find the holes you have and the holes the horse has on a limited scale and then plug the holes and build on the experience. You get to put LOTS of courage pennies in your courage bank!

4. Once you get really good at that 200 feet and pattern, add another 200 foot pattern onto the end of it. Again, if there is an issue, go back to the very beginning and start over. The next time you ride, pick a different set of patterns if you did really well; if not, do the same pattern until you are both great at it.

Edge of Comfort Zone

After getting really comfortable with the video game

method, the final building block for any ride for me was the edge of my comfort zone. I love this one for our first adventures out and about. Pick a spot that you are comfortable with riding to, right at the edge of your comfort zone. It can be a tree, a flower, a fence post, a rock - just pick something that you think, "I would be fine going to that spot," and then pick something a little bit further and go there.

Don't pick something a long way out of your comfort zone, but just outside of it. The idea is like any exercise. You go to where you are comfortable, and then you push it just a little to break down muscle so it can rebuild. This is exactly the same, only we break down fear and rebuild courage.

We have 50 feet between our fence posts, and when I started this process, I was thrilled making it three fence posts and then just turning the corner. I would stop and relax. If things were really good, I would pick another spot that I would be comfortable riding to, and then a little bit further. If at any point, I didn't feel quite as good, or if my horse and I lost connection, I would go back to the video game and return all the way to our starting point and start over. Sometimes, I would even dismount and pick a different spot to get on and start from there, practicing mounting quietly thrown in with riding.

The key with this is to really focus on your boundaries. If you are comfortable with a 100-yard trail ride, don't plan to go for a mile. The plan is to go 110 yards. Every one of these edges you accomplish adds courage points!

PART 5 – PLAN FOR YOUR ADVENTURES

Chapter Fourteen

PLAN FOR COURAGE!

Tomorrow, you will not be the same person you are today; what do you want for the you of tomorrow and your horse?

Saddle up and go. The ultimate goal is being that fearless kid again. They say as you get older, you revert back to your childhood, and in so many ways, I know this deep down to be true.

I have the tools, the building blocks for my courage. I am filling my courage penny bank every day and feeling more and more confident. I am enjoying my horses again, like I used to as a kid. At this point, you now have the tools as well to build your courage back and be riding like that fearless kid you once were.

Build your plan:

- Get yourself healthy. There is so much more joy in riding when you feel good, when your balance and communication with your horse are more like when you were a kid.
- Get your horse healthy. Emotional and physical health for your horse is as important as your health. We are responsible for taking the best care of our partners as we can.
- Develop your amazing vision for your ride to the point where you can feel it through your whole body; be ready for it to show up.

- Two-way communication. Know how to listen to your horse, know how to lead your horse, know that your horse listens to you, know that your horse communicates with you.
- Courage pennies – fill your penny bank. Know the foundation for building your courage.
- Ground play – gives you the opportunity for observation, timing, and developing connection.
- Pre-ride checklist for the rider – know that you are mentally and physically ready for the ride and to be there for your horse.
- Pre-ride checklist for the horse – Know that your horse is connected with you and ready for an adventure.
- Relaxed mounting – you are ready to ride and so is your horse.
- Arena play – make this fun, get creative, build the bond with your horse.
- ADVENTURES – Be that fearless kid again and enjoy your horses.

If you would like more personalized help on your journey, please check out the Rise from Fear to Courage Virtual Clinic information and see if it would be a good fit for you at http:// elisehittinger.com/page/book-bonus

ACKNOWLEDGMENTS

Gratitude

I think of Winnie the Pooh when I think of being grateful. He is my hero at enjoying life and being grateful for what comes his way, especially honey!

There are so many wonderful people that have helped me on my journey that I am thankful for; here is a shout out to a few of them:

- Jazz Napravnik − she gave me the final missing piece. Life Coach with Mindsets Matter.
- Carson James − his methods are all about timing and communication. Soft also means you know when to get firm and how firm.
- Warwick Schiller − he has great exercises broken down into building blocks and the "why" things work as they do within a horse's head.
- Ellicot Miller − patience for my first time out with my new mare and the great exercises he taught us.
- Martha Krejci − without her encouragement and guidance, I would not have ventured into writing a book!

Made in the USA
Monee, IL
12 November 2022

17575478R00046